I0412692

Chronic Anxiety Unreality Sensations and other Odd Symptoms

The Bizarre Manifestations of Panic and
Disordered Anxiousness

By: James M. Lowrance © 2011

2

DEDICATION:

To all of my fellow anxiety disorder sufferers throughout the world. May you find victorious coping skills and regain your quality-of-life by conquering the anxiety symptoms that would steal your joy.

Chronic Anxiety Unreality Sensations and other Odd Symptoms

TABLE OF CONTENTS:

INTRODUCTION:

Beginning in my teen years, I experienced intermittent panic attacks. Previous to this, I suffered prolonged episodes of free-floating anxiety (generalized worry and anxiousness). During my twenties, I found coping skills for my anxiety that were mostly self-taught, although I had seen mental health counselors for short periods of time in my late teens. These sessions were scheduled by my parents; during times I seemed to be lacking the ability to cope as I should, following major events, such as relocating to new schools. This was in the late 1970s and some anxiety therapies, such as Cognitive Behavioral Therapy (CBT), were not as well-developed as they are now.

Additionally, anxiety sufferers also now have the availability of self-treatment methods that have been developed and that can be found online and used in the comfort of one's home. I personally benefited from self-help programs when my anxiety disorder reached a level of severity at age-40, after I developed autoimmune thyroid disease, which caused me a period of hyperthyroidism (overactive thyroid gland).

While I will reference treatments in the chapters of this book, including pharmaceutical and psychiatric therapies, this book will be mostly focused on the subject of anxiety symptom-manifestations. This will include what are known as "unreality symptoms" but I will also add chapters regarding "anxiety sensitization" and "catastrophic thinking".

It is my hope that this information will help anxiety sufferers to understand what is happening to them when they experience these aspects of chronic anxiousness and/or panic attacks. My purpose is to reveal the facts, that these manifestations of severe anxiety and panic are very common but also very treatable and that they will not cause insanity or any real catastrophe. They are in-fact aspects of the anxiety mechanism called the "fight or flight response", which is completely natural and necessary but that can occur out-of-context or at "disordered" times.

In the case of anxiety disorders, knowledge truly is power and gaining an education regarding symptom-manifestations, can lend toward better results for managing these symptoms, as proper treatment is also being administered.

This was key to my own success with gaining coping skills for chronic anxiety symptoms and that I hope to convey through the chapters of this book.

-*Jim Lowrance*

CHAPTER ONE

Understanding Anxiety Depersonalization Symptoms

(Feeling Unreal during the Fight or Flight Response)

When a person is experiencing chronic or severe anxiety symptoms, such as panic attacks or generalized anxiety disorder, they may experience symptoms of depersonalization. The term "depersonalization", is one that describes an anxiety symptom-phenomenon, in which a person feels unreal during intense anxiety episodes or panic attacks.

How Depersonalization Feels

When this unreality anxiety manifestation occurs, a person may feel as if they have become unreal. They temporarily feel as if their personality is no longer present in full-force and that they have somewhat lost a sense of their selves. They may also feel that others around them do not recognize them as fully as they did before they entered into this state of depersonalization.

Some anxiety sufferers describe feeling as if they have become robot-like when this unreality symptom manifests or as if they are watching their selves from outside of their own bodies. They may also feel as if they are experiencing an "identity crises".

Does Depersonalization Indicate Psychosis?

A major fear anxiety disorder sufferers may experience as a result of experiencing depersonalization is that they have entered into a phase of psychosis or insanity however, this is actually not the case and depersonalization actually has nothing to do with a person's sanity. It is in fact simply a manifestation of high levels of anxiety and these episodes are temporary and not a permanent condition. Some sufferers may experience depersonalization episodes frequently or for extended periods of time but this still does not indicate the onset of psychosis because they do not actually lose touch with reality nor do they experience true hallucinations or delusions.

In-short, as unpleasant as this anxiety unreality symptom can be, it is in the "neurosis" category, rather than being in the "psychosis" category. It also cannot crossover into psychosis because these two types of mental/emotional illnesses/disorders have very marked differences between them.

What Triggers Depersonalization?

As previously mentioned, severe anxiety episodes are the trigger however, it is more-specifically a result of the "fight or flight response". This simply refers to the anxiety mechanism that is present in all normal human beings and its purpose is to help one respond to dangers that might manifest.

If for example, a person is attacked by a wild animal, the fight or flight response will cause a sudden release of adrenaline in their body, so that they can run from the danger or defend their selves against it.

However, when this natural mechanism triggers without a real danger being present, such as occurs with anxiety disorders and panic attacks, the perception of the adrenaline surge, may cause strange feelings, such as depersonalization.

How can This Unreality Symptom be Cured?

While there is no actual "cure" for anxiety disorders (immediate full recovery), there are treatments that can help to control symptoms that occur with them, including those of the unreality type. This can be accomplished through prescription drug or psychological therapies, or a combination of both. In many cases, drug therapies can be eliminated, once an anxiety disorder sufferer, has developed coping techniques to help them live normally and fulfill their family, work and educational obligations. Some anxiety disorder sufferers actually cope so well, once they have undergone a therapy, such as "Cognitive Behavioral Therapy" (considered by many psychiatrists as the most successful option) that their quality-of-life is completely restored to pre-neurosis levels over time.

If you suffer from anxiety episodes or symptoms of depersonalization, that you find difficulty coping with or that disrupts and affects your quality-of-life, see your doctor, to discuss with him options and referrals that are available to help you with recovery and coping. Anxiety disorders have a very high treatment success rate and it makes good sense to take advantage of treatments options that are available.

CHAPTER TWO

The Derealization Anxiety Unreality Symptom

(When Surroundings Feel Unreal with Chronic Anxiousness)

Derealization (feeling as if your surroundings are less real) is like depersonalization, in the fact that both are "unreality" anxiety symptoms that may be triggered during episodes of extreme anxiousness or panic attacks.

In the previous chapter, I wrote, on the "unreality anxiety symptom" in-which I discussed the unreality symptom called "depersonalization". As was noted, this symptom may occur in people with triggered anxiousness that is severe or that reaches the panic attack level, causing a sensation of feeling less-real or unreal. **Derealization** is similar but in this case, an anxiety sufferer will experience sensations that cause things around them or their surroundings in-general to feel unreal.

Both of these symptom-manifestations are in the unreality-symptom category and many reputable emotional/mental health sources refer to them in association with anxiety disorders, including the Freedom From Fear Organization (FFF), whose Board of Directors include PhD psychiatrists and medical doctors.

Derealization Does not Indicate Insanity

According to the FFF organization mentioned above, on their page titled "10 Facts of Panic" ---chronic and severe states of anxiety, may produce a variety of strange sensations, including depersonalization and dereralization but these unreality symptoms will not cause anxiety sufferers to go crazy, insane or to enter a state in which they do not return to normal. Anxiety disorders are a type of "neurosis" and they do not result in the onset of psychotic conditions, regardless of the frequency or severity with which one may experience them. Those who suffer chronic anxiety and/or panic attacks can offer their selves reassurance by being reminded of this fact often, when this symptom manifests.

How Derealization Feels

Anxiety disorder sufferers who have written online articles regarding their experiences with this symptom or who have posted their experiences on forums and message boards have stated that derealization causes them to feel as if they are in a dream-like state. Things around them may seem as if they are not really there, even when the physical senses confirm that they are. This is a "sensation" and the person experiencing it, does not actually lose touch with reality during these episodes.

Other experiences described in association with this symptom include feeling a loss in mental-sharpness or what some sufferers describe as "brain fog". Descriptions of brain fog include feeling as if one is looking through a thin veil or through water that is slightly murky. For most anxiety sufferers, this sensation comes in short-term episodes, although they can be prolonged in some cases, especially if depression accompanies chronic anxiety conditions.

According to Dianne Ruth, PhD Psychologist, "Eighty-five percent of anxiety sufferers also struggle with depression."

How Derealization is Treated

This symptom of unreality episodes is treated, by addressing the underlying emotional disorders that are causing it. This can be accomplished through improved lifestyle practices, such as getting proper amounts of rest and sleep, exercising regularly and eating a healthy diet of complex carbohydrates (fruits, vegetables nuts and grains) as opposed to simple carbohydrates (foods with refined sugars in them).

It can also be beneficial for one suffering from emotional imbalances, to stay active in leisure activities and hobbies, to reduce stress-levels.

The most important step in diagnosing and finding treatments for emotional disorder symptoms, such as derealization, is to see a medical doctor or mental health professional for pharmaceutical and/or psychological therapies.

Depending on the severity of an emotional problem, only one type treatment may be needed short-term or a combination of them in more severe cases. Many anxiety disorder sufferers will see successful gains in coping with the aid of treatments and many even regain a pre-illness quality-of-life. Many accomplish this through self-help programs that are also now available and that can be practiced in the comfort of one's home.

Derealization is a very common and highly treatable condition associated with anxiety disorders but it requires effective therapies to be administered.

CHAPTER THREE

Understanding Anxiety Sensitization and Avoiding It

(When Becoming Anxious is Triggered More Easily)

For some anxiety disorder and panic attack sufferers, their anxiety levels can reach an easily triggered state, when they experience extra stress or they are physically unwell or battling fatigue. Anxiety sensitization is a term describing periods of time that anxiety disorder sufferers experience, in which anxiety symptoms are more easily triggered.

Things that can lead to becoming Anxiety Sensitized

While sensitization to anxiety can have different causes among those who experience chronically anxious states, there are common causes that can result in a heightened sensitivity in many of them.

If one experiences added stressors for an extended period of time for example, this can result in becoming more sensitized to anxiety symptoms. If one is not getting proper amounts of sleep or rest, this can become a trigger for becoming more anxious as well. Also, if a person is going through an illness, that places added stress on both the mind and body, this can cause anxiety sensitization to develop as well. These are examples of things that can cause a person to become less-resistant to the onset of highly anxious states and panic attacks.

Recognizing Signs of Increasing Anxiety Levels

Most anxiety disorder patients can easily recognize overt symptoms of increased anxiousness (full blown), which would include things such as increased heart rate, hyperventilation, tingling in the extremities and an increase in sweating. With anxiety sensitization however, the signs and symptoms can be somewhat subtle at first, so that the condition creeps up slowly before the well-recognized symptoms begin to occur.

Some of the signs that can occur when one is heading toward anxiety sensitization, would include feeling fatigued, becoming easily irritable, having feelings of dread toward daily work duties or other everyday tasks that need to be performed and craving more carbohydrates and refined sugars to fill an energy void. Some people refer to a combination of these symptoms, as being "stressed-out". When any of these signs begin to occur, one should take notice and work on methods to avoid an escalation in anxiety symptoms that can follow.

How to Avoid Anxiety Sensitization

While these suggestions may seem simple, they are very effective in helping one to avoid becoming increasingly stressed-out, so that anxiety symptoms are more easily triggered. It is especially important to work on these methods when one is experiencing an illness or problems recovering from mental or physical fatigue.

One major importance is to get adequate rest and sleep, on a daily basis.

Make sure to also take all breaks that are allowed at one's place of occupation and to relax for a few minutes before returning to work duties. If fatigue seems to be developing, this may require stretching-out on a bench or laying one's head on a table during breaks, this should be done, especially during lunch-break, leaving enough time to consume a nutritious mid-day meal.

Also make sure to get a minimum of 8 hours of sleep nightly which can lend-toward avoiding fatigue and stressors that trigger increases in anxiety symptoms.

Reducing or even eliminating any stimulants from the diet can also help. This would include things like caffeine, chocolate, alcohol and refined sugars, which can provide short-term energy but that can also lead to crashes of fatigue and feeling stressed-out afterward.

Replacing these non-nutritious things with healthy foods, such as fruits, vegetables, nuts and grains, can be highly beneficial in battling stress

Leisure time is also essential, which simply means you take time-out during your week, as often as possible, to enjoy things you like doing and that can help you to unwind from the effects of stress. This would include hobbies you enjoy, such as attending sports events, going fishing, painting works of art, or anything else that has a soothing effect on your mind and emotions.

These methods, when practiced regularly, can help one to avoid becoming sensitized to symptoms of chronic or severe anxiety symptoms.

CHAPTER FOUR

Catastrophic Thinking: Unrealistic Anxiety Thoughts

(When Anxiousness Brings Exaggerated Scenarios to Your Mind)

For many anxiety sufferers, their thought patterns can become filled with scenarios of danger and tragedy, which in-turn causes their anxiety levels to increase.

Most people who experience chronic (ongoing) or severe anxiety episodes (i.e. panic attacks or extreme episodes of generalized anxiety), will experience an anxiety symptom manifestation called "catastrophic thinking" (phobic thoughts).

According to Dr. Ron Breazeale a clinical psychologist who has written articles for the Psychology Today online magazine, "Catastrophic thinking can be defined as ruminating about irrational worst-case outcomes".

What is Catastrophic Thinking?

This phenomenon of chronic anxiousness affects the thought patterns of sufferers and is a very common aspect of mood disorders in-general.

When episodes occur, a person will begin to consider worse-case-scenarios that could occur in any given situation. Another term that might be used to refer to these type thought-patterns is to call it "what if thinking".

For example, if a person is experiencing severe anxiety symptoms while in a crowd of people, they might have thoughts such as seeing their self being trampled-on by the bystanders or that they will be violently turned-on by them and attacked.

If for another example, a person is shopping at a supermarket and they begin to feel panicky inside the store, they may begin to picture their self falling to the floor with an episode of hyperventilation, unable to escape through an exit, in order to recover from the anxiety attack.

Chronic Anxious Thoughts can lead to Agoraphobia

While this may sound bizarre to those who do not suffer chronic or severe episodes of anxiety, it is a very real problem to those who do experience them and it reveals an aspect of their disorder that is in need of proper treatment. If catastrophic thinking becomes severe, some sufferers will actually awaken after a night's sleep, immediately contemplating catastrophic scenarios that might occur during their work or other routines of the day. This can eventually contribute to a condition called "agoraphobia", in-which an anxiety sufferer feels the need to be confined inside their home, to avoid these negative possibilities from occurring.

Reassurance for Catastrophic Thinkers

While this aspect of chronic anxiety and panic attacks, is extremely unpleasant, those who suffer with it, should be reassured that it is very common and does not indicate that they will lose their sanity at some point or actually lose self-control while they are out in public or at home with their family.

These are additional fears sufferers may have, regarding these very disturbing thoughts but they are actually harmless in the vast majority of cases, despite being very concerning. Those who experience this manifestation of chronic anxiousness, are often terribly alarmed by some of the thoughts that might enter their minds, such as those in-which they fear they might lose control and become violent toward a loved-one (also a very common fear) but these thoughts are irrational and anxiety sufferers do not actually act upon them. The fact that they are very disturbing is proof that one has no intention of acting upon them, including thoughts of violence or loosing control. Acting-out these types of thoughts is only a possibility, when a person actually enjoys them and purposefully contemplates them, rather than feeling resistant to them and disturbed by them..

The Fight of Flight Response

Many psychiatrists and psychologists have studied the subject of catastrophic thinking in anxiety sufferers and some of their conclusions in regard to this symptom-phenomenon include the fact that the "fight or flight response" causes the mind to search for all possible dangers.

The mind operates at these times, at a high rate of alertness, due to increases in adrenaline levels that are released into the body, via the adrenal glands (two endocrine glands that sit on top of the kidneys). The mind is in-essence considering every possible danger that might be threatening one's safety or that of others around them.

While the triggering of this anxiety mechanism is mis-timed (disordered) and the resulting thoughts can be very disturbing, the response itself is actually natural. It is provided for the purpose of responding to any real dangers that might occur and that require being dealt-with (i.e. fleeing from danger or fighting a real threat). With "anxiety disorders" this natural response occurs at inappropriate times or in a "disordered" fashion.

Treatment

Catastrophic thinking is relieved when the underlying anxiety disorder has been treated. More regarding anxiety treatments, will be addressed in the chapter that follows.

CHAPTER FIVE

Methods for Treating Anxiety Disorders

(Pharmaceutical and Psychiatric Therapies for Chronically Anxious People)

Those who suffer chronic anxiousness should visit their medical doctor or a mental health professional, for referral to proper treatments. There are many prescription medications available for anxiety disorders, including as-needed drugs called benzodiazepines, that can be taken short-term or during anxiety flares and there are long-term medications that can be taken daily, such as SSRI-antidepressants that provide a steady effect to relieve anxiety symptoms.

The following are types of psychotropic drugs (anti-anxiety and antidepressant) that are commonly prescribed to help patients with mood disorder symptoms.

• Paxil (paroxetine)

• Prozac (fluoxetine)

• Zoloft (sertraline) ...

...

- Wellbutrin (buproprion)

- Effexor (venlafaxine)

- Klonopin (clonazepam)

- Ativan (lorazepam)

- BuSpar (buspirone)

- Valium (diazepam)

- Xanax (alprazolam)

For some sufferers, psychiatric therapies can be administered with or without the addition of pharmaceutical drugs. One therapy that has been found to be very effective in treating anxiety conditions is "Cognitive Behavioral Therapy" (CBT) that can be administered by a licensed therapist. Some people with anxiety disorders have successfully self-treated their mood disorder, by use of these type programs/methods, within the privacy of their homes as well. An online search will reveal a number of self-help programs that are available but careful evaluation of each is recommended.

Those that have the involvement or endorsement of mental health professionals are preferable.

Some aspects of CBT that are important parts of the therapy include the following.

CBT helps change the way one thinks about anxiety in general and about the symptoms it causes.

The patient will learn through this aspect of CBT that anxiety itself is a "natural emotion". The unpleasantness of the symptoms in people in whom anxiety has become a "disorder" comes from the fact that this normal emotion can occur out of context or at inappropriate times (disordered). When a patient learns that the emotion he is experiencing is not "strange or foreign," this alone can help toward reducing the fear of the symptoms an anxiety disorder causes.

Once a patient with anxiety accepts the fact that the emotion is natural and that it is supposed to occur at the appropriate times, he can work on steps toward coping with inappropriately triggered anxiety episodes.

**CBT helps to identify "triggers" that cause
anxiety to occur out of context or in a
disordered fashion.**

One way to express this fact to an anxiety sufferer
is to say; "Anxiety is a completely natural and
normal emotion and it is only the timing of it that
has become out of the order it was intended to
happen."

Under normal circumstances, the anxiety emotion
was created to be triggered in order to allow the
one experiencing it to have the sudden added
strength and presence of mind, to flee from
danger or to fight an enemy that has attacked him.
This is the origin of the term triggered-anxiety
that is referred to as the "fight or flight" response.

Some anxiety research groups believe that social
phobia for example, often begins in childhood and
progresses as a person enters adulthood.

The sympathetic nervous system response (yet
another term for the fight or flight response)
begins to trigger inappropriately.

Like other anxiety disorders, the negative responses a person has when feeling anxious about social events or settings they are attending or planning to attend (immediate or anticipated anxiety), becomes more of a learned behavior. A person with Social Anxiety Disorder (SAD) for example, may experience panic attacks when socializing with one or more people or may avoid social settings because of their uncomfortable anxiety symptoms when around people.

Entertainer - Donny Osmond is one famous sufferer of social phobia, with associated panic attacks that he attests to being present beginning in his childhood. He has however, learned to cope with SAD, through drug therapy and Cognitive Behavioral Therapy and has since served as a spokesman for people with anxiety disorders.

CBT Helps one to recognize that anxiety gives added abilities, to perform tasks at hand.

This can be any task that requires what some might also call "intestinal fortitude" - that internal strength we all have and must call upon at times, as it is needed. Everyone has important tasks to perform in their everyday lives.

At times we also experience emergency situations or those with important priorities involved. Firemen must be on alert to put out fires that are called in to them, teachers must have the inspiration to interest their pupils in learning the subjects being studied, and an athlete in a track meet must be ready to run in an attempt to win a race. Without the anxiety emotion, they would not have the added strength and inspiration to accomplish these tasks as successfully.

A person who is called upon to make a public speech for example, needs that extra inspiration to bring forth his spoken points more powerfully and with conviction. Anxiety is what adds to this experience and helps them to accomplish this. The butterflies in the stomach and sweaty hands can actually be a sign that one is about to make a powerful presentation and not that they are about to run off of the stage due to stage-fright and so, it is all in how one perceives it. You can make anxiety responses work for you or work against you. Will you see it as positive energy to help inspire you or as fear that is holding you back? That is the question.

Herein lays the secret to these previously described aspects of Cognitive Behavioral Therapy; the way in which one perceives the anxiety they are experiencing and their response to it!

CHAPTER SIX

The Differences between Anxiety Neurosis and Psychosis Disorders

(Knowing Anxiety will not Cause You Insanity)

While the symptoms of anxiety and panic attacks can be extremely unpleasant and disrupting to a person's life, they will not progress to loss of sanity or to becoming psychotic. As I have mentioned in previous chapters, a common fear of anxiety sufferers, is that their mood disorder will progress to a state of psychosis, meaning a condition in which one begins to lose touch with reality and to hallucinate or to become delusional.

Neurosis Statistics

Anxiety is actually in the "neurosis" category and some estimates, including those published by the National Institute of Mental Health (NIMH) in the U.S., state that over 18% of the adult American population suffers from anxiety disorders. The statistics for adolescence age individuals (ages 13 to 18), is even higher, being estimated at over 25%.

When combined, this is a very significant portion of the general population. When statistics for non-bipolar depressive disorders is added-in (i.e. clinical depression and seasonal affective disorder) which often crossover with anxiety conditions, the overall statistics for mood disorders in-general is at a very high prevalence.

Psychosis Statistics

When statistics for disorders of psychosis, which includes schizophrenia, severe types of bipolar disorder and borderline personality disorders are compared to that of neurosis, the prevalence of them is very small in comparison. The U.S. NIMH for example, estimates that schizophrenia affects an estimated 1.1% of the general adult population. Bipolar disorder is estimated by them, to affect approximately 2.6% of the adult U.S. population and borderline personality disorder is estimated to affect approximately 1.6% of the general adult population. All combined, the statistics for psychotic disorders does not even reach that of even one type of anxiety disorder, of which there are many.

This includes Social Anxiety Disorder, Panic Disorder, Generalized anxiety Disorder, Post Traumatic Stress Disorder and Agoraphobia.

Neurosis does not become Psychosis

If people who suffer anxiety disorders and non-bipolar clinical depression, were at risk for developing conditions of psychosis, these statistics <u>would not</u> be at such wide variance. The fact is that neurosis and psychosis are in two distinct categories, one being of exclusively an emotional imbalance (neurosis) and the other being of actual mental illness that may or may not have significant emotional aspects involved with it (psychosis with or without anxiety or depression).

With psychosis, people actually experience episodes or ongoing delusions and hallucinations but with neurosis, this aspect is not present. Mood disorders can cause sensations of unreality, such as depersonalization and derealization but these feelings do not cause sufferers of them to actually lose touch with reality or to become delusional or to hallucinate in the true sense of these words.

It is important for sufferers of anxiety neurosis who fear the onset of a psychotic disorder, to understand the differences between the two, which can help them to overcome this fear.

CHAPTER SEVEN

Anxiety and Heart Palpitations

(Racing, Skipping, Fluttering and Thumping Heartbeats)

A medical doctor should be consulted when one is experiencing an irregular heartbeat of any type. While most heart palpitations are benign (harmless) some can indicate a structural problem within the heart muscle that requires treatment. With this disclaimer added, I will also point out that heart palpitations are extremely common among anxiety disorder patients.

Skips and Thumps

The heart rhythm occurrences called PVCs (Premature Ventricular Contractions) and PACs (Premature Atrial Contractions), which are felt by the one experiencing them, as a pause in the heartbeat, followed by a thump sensation in the chest, neck or abdomen, are very common, especially in people with chronic anxiety or stress.

Due to the fact that they are experienced by such a large percent of the general population, huge numbers of posts regarding them can be found on heart-health medical forums online. In some cases, patients are warning their fellow-patients, about the risk these palpitations have for causing eventual heart failure or sudden death from cardiac arrest. This type of information does however need to be seasoned with some perspective, based on reliable medical information, so as not to be ambiguous regarding realistic risk factors. Such statements, taken out-of-context, can contribute to an anxiety disorder referred to as "cyberchondria", which is a very real problem that can result from imbalanced online medical search (lacking proper perspective).

Most Patients Palpitations Report Good Heart Health

According to information I found on reputable medical sources, regarding these common heart palpitations, heart disease is not the most common cause of PVCs/PACs. If that were the case, the estimated 50% of the general population, believed to have relatively frequent PVCs/PACs, would all be walking around with heart disease.

I have seen literally 1,000s of posts by frequent PVC/PAC sufferers, whose cardiologists ruled out structural heart disease of any kind via complete workups (i.e. stress test/EKG and echocardiograms) and yet they experience these highly concerning pause-thumps, on a daily bases. Many relate having experienced them since their childhood and yet they were still given a clean bill of heart health in their 30s, 40s or 50s, by their cardiologists.

Cardiomyopathy and Heart Palpitations

As far as cardiomyopathy goes (weakening of the heart muscle -- also called "heart failure"), PVCs/PACs should not place any more stress and wear on the heart than would normal activities that increase the heart rate (i.e. exercise, excitement and sex), because the premature beat that happens with PVCs/PACs, is simply that...a double-beat. This would be equal to two heartbeats that simply occur closer together.

People who do develop cardiomyopathy following years of constant PVCs/PACs, likely had a propensity or predisposition toward developing it and the palpitations were simply a contributing factor.

I will add that in rare cases, it's possibly a direct cause of heart failure but likely far more of a possibility in senior age people and/or in those who already have serious co-morbid health problems. I base this on my search/research on many medical websites that specialize in heart health information.

I recently viewed a YouTube video by Dr. Stephen Sinatra, a Board Certified Cardiologist, in which he states these facts, plus admits the he also experiences PVCs, as did many of his fellow students, which they discovered when they were studying for their medical credentials. He mentions "stress" in the video, as a precipitating factor for the occurrence of these palpitations, occurring in students pursuing their educational degrees to practice professional medicine.

Is there Diagnostic Value in Common Irregular Heartbeats?

Far too many reputable cardiologists are stating that their many years as practitioners in this field of specialty have shown that these irregular heartbeats are very common and very rarely pose a health-threat to otherwise healthy people (some cardiologists even call them "normal").

They add statements to this fact, saying to the effect that PVCs/PACs rarely have any diagnostic significance and many of these doctors admit to experiencing them their selves. Keep in mind that we are talking about irregular heart beats, rather than chronic arrhythmias (an ongoing rather than intermittent change in cardiac rhythm).

Anxiety: A Major Trigger for Palpitations

I also want to add the fact, that people, who anticipate PVCs/PACs, due to their fear of them, are actually contributing to more of them (certainly not their fault but a natural response). Also, when one occurs, it tends to cause a quick surge of adrenaline in the body, due to the anxiety these palpitations may cause (fight or flight response) and this will instantly trigger succeeding PVCs/PACs, possibly several of them in a row (PVC Complexes).

For this reason, people who are under chronic stress or anxiety can experience them with more frequency than do people who have other triggers for them (i.e. caffeine, following exercise or lack of sleep).

Heart Flutters

Most people experience what they perceive as an occasional skipped heartbeat or a pause in heart rhythm as previously mentioned. Many times this will be followed by an extra-hard heartbeat or what one might call a thump in their chest or a flip-flopping sensation.

In some people, these strange heartbeats (palpitations) are also accompanied by a fluttering feeling in the chest that may last for a few seconds at a time.

These sensations can be very concerning to the one experiencing them however, in the vast majority of cases, they are neither harmful nor dangerous and they do not indicate that heart disease is present or developing.

Of course at the same time, they can indicate the manifestation of a health condition needing treatment (either heart-related or indirectly affecting the heart) and so it is always wise to have them evaluated by a medical doctor.

Other Contributing Factors for Heart Palpitations

In addition to stress and anxiety, medical sources, including the U.S. National Institutes of Health, state that these common heart palpitations can occur during or following hard physical exercise, such as an aerobic work-out or following a brisk walk or a jog.

Hormonal imbalances can contribute to heart palpitations as well, including thyroid disorders and changes in sex hormone levels, such as those that occur with menopause, pregnancies and menstrual cycles in women. Some medical experts also believe that untreated hypertensive conditions (high blood pressure) can also contribute to heart palpitations.

According to many medical sources on heart-health subjects, a condition called "Mitral Valve Prolapse" can also be a factor in heart palpitations (also a common factor in anxiety symptoms). This common but usually benign "click-murmur" effects from 15 to 20 percent of the general population to some degree, according to some medical statistics.

Yet others, who experience these strange heartbeat sensations, will not identify any particular trigger for them but they simply experience them for unknown reasons.

Tachycardia

Of all the palpitations that anxiety disorder sufferers will commonly notice, the most common one would likely be tachycardia (rapid heartbeat). This is simply a response by the heart and other muscles in the body, to increased levels of adrenaline, resulting from the fight or flight response. For some anxiety patients, tachycardia is a daily occurrence or relatively ongoing for them.

As has been stated regarding the other types of heart palpitations that have been discussed, tachycardia does not lead to a heart attack or heart failure in otherwise healthy people. I have spent less time on this type palpitation due to the common knowledge of the fact that a racing heart is so very common with anxiety and panic attacks.

My Personal Experience with Heart Skips

When I was a teenager, I first experienced episodes of rapid and/or skipped heartbeats, which were very concerning to me. These would occur in phases but with some frequency, continuing into my twenties. I would then have years at a time that would pass, during my thirties and early forties, in which the heart-skips would only occur rarely and sometimes, I would only feel one occur and afterward none would occur for weeks or months at a time (at least none I could actually feel).

Now in my late forties, I have had a few phases of these but I have identified very definite triggers for mine, which include consuming chocolate or beverages containing caffeine, at any level above small amounts. Moderate to excessive consumption of these and refined sugars, will often set off a phase of heart-skips for me. My suspicion is that this is due to my already having a propensity toward being stressed and anxious, which can be exacerbated by stimulants. I have experienced anxiety disorder symptoms, including occasional panic attacks, at various points in my life, as mentioned in the introduction of this book.

I also tend to push myself too-hard in my work activities, rather than taking needed rest periods and I will become stressed-out, resulting in the heart palpitations. Lacking proper amounts of sleep can contribute to them in my case as well.

IN CONCLUSION:

There are many symptoms-manifestations of chronic anxiety and panic attacks, some being more odd and unusual than others. All of these are easily attributed to the anxiety mechanism -- the fight or flight response and all of them can be significantly improved and even alleviated with proper treatment for underlying anxiety disorders. It is my sincere hope that the preceding chapters have helped readers who may suffer chronic anxiety, by arming them with the knowledge that they are not alone in experiencing their symptoms.

It is also my hope that they will realize that the more unusual manifestations of their anxiety are actually common and in the vast majority of cases, are neither harmful nor dangerous. Gaining this knowledge, in addition to receiving proper treatment, can contribute greatly toward overcoming "disordered anxiety", so that the fight or flight response is better controlled (placed back into proper order) and works for the person with anxiety, rather than against them.

-Jim Lowrance

www.ingramcontent.com/pod-product-compliance
Lightning Source LLC
Chambersburg PA
CBHW061225280526
45784CB00006B/2637